BECOMING
AN ANCESTOR

Also by Lucille Lang Day

POETRY

The Curvature of Blue
Infinities
Wild One
Fire in the Garden
Self-Portrait with Hand Microscope

POETRY CHAPBOOKS

Dreaming of Sunflowers: Museum Poems
God of the Jellyfish
The Book of Answers
Lucille Lang Day: Greatest Hits, 1975–2000

MEMOIR

Married at Fourteen: A True Story

CHILDREN'S BOOK

Chain Letter

SCIENCE EDUCATION

*How to Encourage Girls in Math and Science: Strategies
for Parents and Educators* (coauthor)

*SEEK (Science Exploration, Excitement, and Knowledge):
A Curriculum in Health and Biomedical Science
for Diverse 4th and 5th Grade Students* (editor)

Family Health and Science Festival: A SEEK Event (editor)

BECOMING AN ANCESTOR

POEMS BY LUCILLE LANG DAY

Červená Barva Press

Červená Barva Press
P.O. Box 440357
West Somerville, MA 02144-3222

http://www.cervenabarvapress.com
Bookstore: http://www.thelostbookshelf.com

Cover photographs, grandparents of Lucille Lang Day:
Top row: Ada Peckham Lang (ca. 1874 – 1952)
and William Lang (ca. 1870 – 1958)
Bottom row: Ebenezer Ellis Bumpus (1875 – 1940)
and Emma Hazard Bumpus (née Rachel Emma Sampson, 1881 – 1919)

Author photo by Hilary Brodey

Cover design and production by Jan Thyer
Page design, composition, and typography by Dickie Magidoff

Library of Congress Control Number (LCCN): 2015945294

ISBN: 978-0-9861111-6-7

For my daughters,
Liana (1963-2013) and Tamarind

and my grandchildren,
Brandon, Sabine, Autumn, and Devlin

Contents

Becoming an Ancestor

We do not live in our own time alone;
we carry our history within us.

— Jostein Gaarder, *Sophie's World*

Journeys

For my parents, Evelyn and Richard Lang

The past is never dead. It's not even past.
—William Faulkner, *Requiem for a Nun*

Rivers glitter. A warm rain
spurs hunter-gatherers to migrate
out of Africa, past the Red Sea
toward unnamed fields and seasons.
Their descendants polish tools,
plant peas and wheat, which starts
the Neolithic Revolution. It says so
in all the rings my mother gave me
of mitochondrial DNA.

Glaciers take up so much water
my ancestors can walk across
the Bering Strait. Through centuries
they walk without a map or compass
all the way to Massachusetts,
arriving thousands of years before
my Anglo-Saxon forebears take
their gods and goddesses to Sussex,
long before John and Peter
de Peckham join the third Crusade.

In a heaving sea John Howland
is swept off the *Mayflower*. He grabs
a halyard. The crew snags
his clothes with a boat hook
to drag him back to the deck.
In my double helices he feasts
with Wampanoags on venison,

roast goose, wild turkey, pumpkins,
squash, plums and berries
under oaks with scarlet leaves.

John Peckham renounces his father,
Lord of the Manor in Sussex, wakes
on a ship, crowded with prisoners,
driven by the wind's stiff whip
toward Massachusetts Bay.

A German baron loses a battle
against King Wilhelm. His son
and daughter-in-law flee. Their son,
Bill Lang, finds his way to California,
proposes to Ada Peckham on a boat
bobbing in the middle of a lake.

With every breath I take, filling
the elegant, finely branched trees
of my lungs with oxygen, my mother's
mother dies again of pneumonia
in Massachusetts in the flu epidemic
of 1918, and my mother comes over
mountains, rivers and plains
to California, where she grows up
to marry Bill and Ada's son.

Over and over, in my round and spindly
cells where the past softly breathes,
my mother, who told no one
she was descended from the Pilgrims
and the People of the First Light,
who brought them corn and deer,
names me "Light." Over and over,
I ask myself, Where am I going?
How will I know when I'm there?

My Mother's Mixer

An ivory KitchenAid with a deep glass bowl,
it had a black knob on top with ten settings
to rotate the heart-shaped beater.
Cookie recipes began with butter and sugar,
creamed. My mother threw in lots of stuff:
to three cups of flour she'd add
one cup of anger and two of love,
a pinch of prejudice, belief in God
but not in saints. Her mixer mixed it up:
a passion for clothes and bingo,
eggs, vanilla, talkativeness, secrecy,
lemon rind, desire to hide the past.
She handed each ingredient to me,
her helper, as I sat at the breakfast table.
"Add a teaspoon of cinnamon," she'd say.
"Fold in the raisins. Don't lie or wear
your skirt too short." When I asked
about her childhood in Massachusetts
before her grandparents took her away,
she'd say, "Don't ask so many questions."
Wanting to please, I blended everything
the way she told me to, then licked
the beater. I already knew her mother died,
her father couldn't raise her and her sister,
and her grandmother was cruel. The recipe
was never quite right: she always handed me
too much butter or sugar, too little truth.

Figurines

They seemed old-fashioned when I was a child,
as they curtseyed above the fireplace.
I didn't like them, but my mother was beguiled

by the way they cocked their heads and softly smiled
in their flowing gowns, ermine muffs and lace.
They seemed old-fashioned when I was a child,

with their parasols, bouquets, blue eyes so mild,
and curls adorning each bone china face.
I didn't like them, but my mother was beguiled.

I yearned for all things new and free and wild,
not Dinky Do's and Genevieve's prim grace.
They seemed old-fashioned when I was a child

from their petticoats to how their hair was styled,
but now I keep them in an oak-trimmed case
in the dining room. My husband's not beguiled

by the bows and hats and fans I once reviled.
In my home, my mother left her trace
in figurines old-fashioned to a child.
She cherished them, and now I am beguiled.

I Always Knew It

I knew it at four when I ran for the creek
every chance I got
and my uncle called me "the wild Indian"
as I slid down the bank,
then leapt from stone to stone
to reach the other side.
I knew it when my parents threatened
to give me back to the Indians
if I didn't behave.
I didn't care. I wanted
to meet the Indians.
I knew it as I rooted for them
in all the old Westerns
and lamented when they lost
and were cast as the bad guys
again and again. I knew it
when my Native American studies
teacher said, "I think you're an Indian,"
and when my aunt told my mother,
"Tell her the truth. Tell her
what she wants to hear."
I knew it at twenty-three
as I stood at a dusty crossroad
on the Rosebud Reservation.
It was stamped on my mother's
high cheekbones and woven
in her dark hair. It was clear
as the difference between
flat redwood needles
and the scales of a giant sequoia,
clear as the difference

between the musical
chirps of Wilson's warbler
and the soft, hoarse whistle
of Brewer's blackbird. I could feel
the People of the First Light stirring
inside me with each contraction
of actin and myosin fibers
in all my muscles, with each
nerve impulse as sodium
rushed into my neurons
and potassium rushed out.
I knew it all along. I knew it
before I could prove it
with a DNA test, long before
I'd heard of Wampanoags. I always
knew it. By the stick-like body
of the tule bluet, the silence
of the lynx chasing rabbits for food,
the silvery needles of Sitka
spruce, and the yodel-like
laugh of the common loon,
I knew it was true.

Glass Animals

The earth hugs pale roots
crawling toward bedrock.
Underground there are
whole cities. I dream
I live there.

*

A woman with no coat
waits in light rain.
Trees after rain
wear beaded cloaks, bend
toward invisible fires.

*

My grandmother's closet
was filled with long
beaded black dresses
a widow would wear.
At four I wanted
to wear them, play dress-up.

*

Sometimes I feel
invisible as roots
or rain that does not fall,
my arms and legs entangled
in snaky vines I
can't cut or see.

*

My grandmother, who saw
a dancing bear
on her way to school, burned

my grandfather's letters
written in German.

*

I wanted a puppy.
My grandfather bought
my drawings for pennies,
nickels, dimes. After
my grandmother died
he gave me glass animals.

*

The day the gerbil died
I dreamed I broke
a glass with my teeth.
I still have two little pigs,
the pink-nosed skunks,
the fawn that sleeps.

Cosmology Lesson

When I was four, my friend Diane
said her cousin Claire thought
she was the center of the universe
and everything existed just for her.
I was stunned. "I thought I was
the center of the universe," I said,
my lip starting to quiver. "We all
start out thinking that," Diane, age nine,
who'd taught me how to add and read,
explained as I burst into tears, scared
in a brand new way. Her mother said,
"She's just a little girl. Don't make
her cry," but it was too late. Birds
were already singing for someone else,
maybe themselves. Even my parents
and my toys no longer belonged
only to me. The sun, moon
and stars trembled as they turned
away, leaving me alone, small
as a bit of broken shell on a beach,
helpless before the gathering waves.

Disneyland, 1956

More than anything, I wanted to be
in my dad's home movie,
whizzing down the Matterhorn,

flying high on Dumbo,
sailing in the sky like Peter Pan,
falling like Alice into Wonderland;

but Uncle Bob bet Dad
a hundred dollars he couldn't resist
including me, so Dad aimed

the camera at the river, caught all
those crocodiles and hippopotami,
mouths open wide, on the safari ride,

Indians dancing in Frontier Land,
strangers at Sleeping Beauty's castle,
but he lost the bet anyhow.

Maybe Dad thought Uncle Bob
wouldn't see me spinning
in the tea cup. He had no kids

of his own to teach
about survival in a magical world
where ducks and mice can talk,

trains stop in the past, and a girl
can step inside an atom.
The trick is not to vanish.

Great-Grandmother

For Mariam Gertrude Peckham, 1846-1914

In autumn she picked apples, packed the good ones in barrels,
and husked corn on the back porch, storing
some for winter fodder, grinding the rest for johnnycake.

She piled yellow pumpkins in the cellar
while the children gathered walnuts, butternuts
and chestnuts—mostly to sell, but plenty to eat.

Sweet cider, which filled her china pitcher
through the fall, was kept
for vinegar when it started to work.

On snowy nights Mariam sat at her desk
and wrote that women should wear pants in public,
attend the universities, and vote.

It was often after midnight when she went upstairs
to the room where Henry was sleeping
under a star-patterned quilt.

He'd wake when she crawled in.
Splinters of moonlight pierced the shutters
clattering in wind.

In March, snow melting, Henry tapped
the maple trees and took the sap inside
for Mariam to strain and boil down.

She sold her articles to magazines,
sewed for neighbors, and ran a millinery shop,
all the while dreaming of a world where women

could enter any profession.

She told Henry, and he nodded as she tacked
a red silk rose to a hat.

My Grandmother's Painting

For Ada Peckham Lang, ca. 1874-1952

Two peach-colored roses disintegrate
on the table. A third hangs
limply from the vase. Three more,
though aged, remain standing.
The upper right corner is olive green,
the lower left black—a place
where light doesn't enter, dark
as wet earth on a grave. She painted it
at finishing school, Chamberlain Institute,
back when she rode a bicycle.
When I asked why she didn't paint others,
my aunt said she threw them away.

She had myasthenia gravis, which causes
muscle weakening. At the end
you can't swallow or breathe.
Her doctor, who misdiagnosed it, ordered
electroshock. It killed her. My father
had the same disease. *Reader's Digest*
rejected his stories. He took
photographs all his life but framed
only one, "Reflections: 1978":
under Mt. Tamalpais, just
after sunset, multicolored needles
of light pierce San Francisco Bay.

My grandmother taught school
until my granddad proposed on a lake.
After painting, she tried writing,
kept diaries for sixteen years.

They're now in my closet:
all her records of sunshine, rain,
dates when planes crashed
in the bay, and rousing quotations
such as O.S. Marden's
"Don't wait for extraordinary
opportunities. Seize common
occasions and make them great."

Clouds

My father photographed red-orange plumes
fanning from the horizon. Click.
Cumulus creatures tumbling
in azure pastures. Click.
Feathers and turrets, gold satin
stratus sheets. Click. Click.

He couldn't capture the taste
of chocolate, the call of a warbler,
or even my mother's touch, the weight
of her hand on his arm. His photos
don't show what happens
when the cloud base lowers:
rain becomes heavy,
pummeled by fists of wind.

Dad and the Gypsy

My dad has fallen for a gypsy woman
with olive skin, red nails and shining eyes.
Her kiss at Safeway took him by surprise
as he studied the label of a soup can.

She said, "I'm sorry to hear your wife died.
We ought to go to dinner and a show."
That sounded good. Although he didn't know
who she was, it was easy to decide

to write his number on a slip of paper
and hand it to her. The next time they met,
they saw *Showboat* and shared a banana split.
"I'm an interior decorator,"

she said, "and I've designed three hotel rooms
in Reno. Let's go pick up my check.
We can share a room—a king-sized bed, deck
and kitchenette—just like a bride and groom.

There's just one thing I hope you'll understand.
I need to borrow some money from you
before we leave: fifteen thousand will do.
When I get paid, I'll give you thirty grand."

Dad replied, "Ask them to mail your check,"
but he wanted to hold hands and kiss again.
He loved her leopard dress, dark hair, smooth skin,
and thought her crystal ball might bring him luck.

For dinner on a moonlit night in June,
she cooked shrimp, and he brought chardonnay.

She said, "Dick, I don't want to dismay
you, but I need an operation soon."

She showed him a cigar box filled with cash.
"I have thirty grand, but the docs want
twenty more." He loved her jasmine scent,
but caught a sudden whiff of rotting fish.

Her messages don't ask for his forgiveness.
He hasn't answered yet, but he still yearns
for all the little things one never learns
to do without: red nails, a leopard dress.

The Man Who Believed in Santa Claus

We always ate lots of popcorn and candy
at the movies, defying my mother.
On summer weekends we rode
the merry-go-rounds at Tilden Park
and the Santa Cruz Boardwalk. Once
he threw the ring in the clown's mouth
as his wooden horse bobbed up and down,
and he demanded a free ride because
that was the deal when he was a boy.
I had to beg him not to use up all
our fireworks before dark on the Fourth
of July, and to wait until Christmas
to open his presents. I set an example
by not opening mine. He made me mad,
refusing to admit that Santa wasn't real.
I thought he was lying, not wanting
me to grow up, but decades later,
after my mother died, he kept two
Santa dolls on the mantel over the fireplace
year-round. One, with a cotton beard,
winked in his red felt suit, fur-trimmed hat,
white boots. The other, a china figurine
waving hello with his right hand,
spun on a music box that played
"Jingle Bells." By the worn chair
where Santa's advocate always sat,
he kept the *New York Sun's* 1897 response
to Virginia O'Hanlon's question,
"Is there a Santa Claus?" "Yes, Virginia,
there is a Santa Claus," the *Sun* replied:
the things we cannot see are more real

than the ones we can, and only faith,
poetry, love and romance can briefly
push the veil aside. The man who believed
in Santa had congestive heart failure
and myasthenia gravis, and his heart fluttered
like sheets on a line. We buried his ashes
at Mountain View, but when I close my eyes,
I see him in his knit cap, riding shotgun
at Santa's side, helping steer eight reindeer
past the moon, in a starry winter sky.

Puzzle

The Dreamer's Trunk

His white beard eddies and flows.
In his yellow gown he might
be Santa in his nightclothes. I think
of elves and the two Santa figurines
my dad displayed year-round.

The bell at the tip of his cap,
striped yellow and black, touches
his shoulder. He wears spectacles,
holds a small cart with a yellow sail
and dangling block and key.

His slipper, with its colorful map,
is open in back, curves up
in front. His long belt is studded
with keyholes. A trunk spills over
with toys: a top, a horn, a teddy bear.

A golden angel hovering with a trumpet
reminds me of my mother's angels:
white plastic ones with pointed wings,
cone-shaped ones with round
wooden heads, red mesh ones,

a white wax one with a wick
on top of her head, a little china one
with long, painted eyelashes, her arms
curved to wrap around a candle.
I've also kept necklaces I'll never wear

and the marbles my dad played with
as a boy. I spread out the pieces,
remembering Christmas morning,
my red stocking with the white cuff
stuffed with candy canes and little dolls.

So many dents and knobs don't fit.
I can't make sense of anything:
the chipmunk in its cape by the door
to the trunk, the latch, this life,
the fading into black, the book of dreams.

Aunt Ethel, Please

Aunt Ethel, please tell them you're not confused.
You know who you are and that you live
on the tenth floor of Westlake Christian Terrace.
I know you're 92 and this is hard, but please
tell them I'm your niece and you're my mother's twin,
born on Perry Hill in Acushnet, Massachusetts,
not New Bedford, as my mother always said.
You're in the hospital, but you're not sick.
The problem is you don't know what day it is.
You look in the bathroom for milk and cheese
and swear that cake is ham and peas are bread.
Tell them you married Richard Hallam,
a Navy man, on Bastille Day in 1948,
that you played bingo with him every week
at the Officers' Club at Alameda Naval Air Station
and he made delicious stews and chocolate cakes.
"Did you finish your ice cream?" you ask.
"I hope you saved some for the little girl,"
but there's no ice cream here, no little girl.
Aunt Ethel, I want to take you back
to your apartment decked with knick-knacks
and greeting cards collected through the years,
but the doctors think you're too confused
to be alone. I don't want to leave you here,
all hunched and small. Please sit as straight
as you can and tell them tea is tea, the food
too bland. Do it for me. Tell me who I am.

Pilgrimage

Grandfather, I have come to Acushnet,
Land of the Cushenas, settled by the Pilgrims in 1639
and bought for 30 yards of cloth, 8 moose skins,
15 axes, 15 hoes, 15 pairs of breeches, 8 blankets,
2 kettles, 1 cloak, 2£ in Wampum, 8 pairs of stockings,
8 pairs of shoes, 1 iron pot, and 10 shillings.

To find you, I have crossed clear skies
and oceans of clouds, rising and falling
in massive white waves. Years, decades,
nearly a century stretched between us
like a rickety bridge, threatening to collapse
before I could reach you.

It's been eighty years since you waved at the train
taking my twelve-year-old mother
and her twin sister to live in California
with their mother's adoptive parents.
When you said good-bye on the platform,
did you know they'd soon have new names?

The first time I saw your name,
Ebenezer Ellis Bumpus, I laughed out loud,
thinking of Ebenezer Scrooge, Ichabod Crane
and country bumpkins. How could I have known
of Nathan Cobb Bumpus, Rowland Sturtevant Bumpus,
and your pride in your old New England name?

Grandfather, I have come to Acushnet
on a bright September day
and knelt at the grave where you lie
beside Emma Hazard Bumpus,

half-Wampanoag orphan, and your three children
who didn't live to see their second birthdays.

My mother never told me the color
of your hair and eyes. She told no one your name.
I think she must have loved you,
but it was an unbearable weight,
and now that weight has passed to me
like a suitcase too heavy to carry.

Ebenezer Ellis Bumpus, what did you look like?
What did you do at the shoe factory?
What gave you joy? I have stood
on the wooded street where you lived,
and now I'll search until I find you beyond
forests, so dense in my dreams.

Return to Acushnet

To my mother

I've found the town where you were born,
whose name you never told me,
and met the family you were torn from,
not as a baby
but as a child old enough to know
your mother was dead,
your father letting you go.

I ran an ad to find descendants
of your father's sisters.
One lived in a log cabin in Acushnet
amid red maples, weeds, abandoned cars.
Her crazy brother lived alone next door
in the shingled farmhouse that belonged
to your grandparents when they were young,
raising children, chickens, pigs and cows.

The fireflies in Massachusetts winked and glowed
in the elms in early summer,
constellations appearing and disappearing
like memories amid the leaves.

Out back, a tractor sat rusting in tall grass—
the carcass of an animal,
fossilized, extinct. The barn
had fallen down the year before. The porch
that used to wrap around the house
was gone. A notice in the window said
"Condemned." The once grand stairs inside
were carpeted with dust. Paint peeled

from the walls; boxes, bags and garbage
filled the rooms. I went upstairs:
I had to see it all. Pine floorboards
were loose, cobwebs everywhere.

I closed my eyes and saw bright quilts
where long ago your father's sisters slept.
When I came back down,
Cousin Ken stared straight ahead
in the kitchen, trembling from his drugs.

Mother—your father, aunts and uncle,
all long gone, are listed on the Internet.
Imagine it! Ernestine, born first,
watched the little ones: Valetta,
Harriet and Mabel, who quilted, sang,
and put on plays; Rowland and your father,
Ebenezer, who liked to trick the girls.
The night I visited the house
where they were born, your father
appeared in a dream, lithe
and handsome, with his big mustache.

"Go back to California," he said.
"I'll come visit you." I think he wanted
to stand beside me, watching
a Western gull, its pink feet
skimming the crests of the Pacific,
hear Hutton's vireo call
from the top of a California oak, wrap
his taut arms tight around us both
like a shipwrecked sailor clinging to the mast,
but I knew in the end he'd let go.

John Billington

First person executed in Plymouth, 1630

They say I am foul-mouthed,
a miscreant and a knave. So be it.
It's better than being a slave
to Bradford, Standish, Winslow
and all the God-obsessed folks
who grovel before their Lord
each day in the dirt-floor huts
lined up in this dreary outpost.

My young son Francis marked
our arrival in this wilderness
by firing my musket once
near an open barrel of gunpowder
onboard the *Mayflower.* Nearly
blew the damn ship up! But
I signed the Compact, vowing
allegiance to our "civil body politic."

John Jr. wandered into the woods
and was captured by natives,
lived with them a month. What boy
worth his salt has never run away?
What man worth his bows to authority?
Let us not fear the devil, I say,
but demand the freedom to gamble
on Christmas, dance and drink whiskey.

Elizabeth Contemplates Her Will

Elizabeth Tilley Howland, 1607-1687

Thirteen years old, I survived
sixty-five awful days
under the leaking deck

of that stinking ship
where people's gums bled
and breath reeked,

teeth wobbling in their mouths.
John fell into the sea
during a storm, but luckily

was hauled back on board.
My parents, aunt and uncle
endured the trip

only to die that first winter
in Plymouth. Three years later
I married John.

We had ten children,
and I helped him plant
fields of wheat and corn.

Now he's gone, and I
must decide which
of my children and their children,

who number eighty-eight,
will get *Mr. Tindale's Works,*
Willson on the Romanes,

my sheets and pillowbeers,
rugs and blankets,
iron pot and pothooks,

brass kettle, cupboard,
andirons, chest, trammel
and land with the meadow.

Who will read my great Bible
and small one? Who
will sleep in my feather bed,

feed my sheep, wear
my linen and woolen clothes,
use my pans to bake their bread?

Edward and Hannah Bumpus

When Edouad Bompasse got to Plymouth
in 1621, the other Pilgrims called him
Edward Bumpus, but why complain
after long weeks at sea on the *Fortune*
and reaching a continent with no king
or Pope, where the land was almost free?

At first he planted Indian style—
in circles like small volcanoes, three
feet apart, with corn seeds at the center.
When he'd saved enough, he bought
an ox and plow, planted wheat and barley
in long straight rows like an Englishman
to sell to newcomers up north
at Massachusetts Bay. Hannah kept
a garden where she tended peas,
cabbages, radishes, carrots, garlic, onions,
melons, artichokes, skirrets and leeks.

She bore twelve children in a house
built around a great brick chimney.
There wasn't much to do in Plymouth
but work and pray, so if the family
members weren't always dutiful
who could blame them? Except, of course,
the preachers and magistrates,
who ordered son John publicly whipped
for *idle and lasivius behavior*,
Edward Jr. for *stricking and abusing
his parents*, a lenient punishment
because *hee was crasey brained*.

A narrow, winding staircase ascended
from the entry hall to the chamber
where Hannah made love with Thomas Bird
in her 55th year, until they too were caught
and whipped. Edward Sr. took her back,
and she set violets and daffodils among
the onions for her forty-eight grandchildren
to pick, intermixed lilies and daisies
with parsnips, and stitched a new dress.

John and Sarah Bumpus, 1692

When the witch trials started up north
in Salem, Sarah was already round
with Jeremiah, their ninth child.
John thought back to when he was whipped
for idleness and flirtation as a young man
and shuddered, thinking how much
worse the allegation might have been.

Now even Governor Phips's wife
and shipmaster John Alden, son of John
and Priscilla, stood accused. Would
it never end? The Andover witches
all offered the same account: the devil
was a small black man who made them
renounce their baptism and sign his book.

Sarah hoped to God no witches would
ever be found in Plymouth. The baby
was due in August, the time to cut
wheat and rye. Had it been a mistake
for the Old Colony to join Massachusetts,
where the witches flew and cried? She
wondered, throwing corn to dappled swine.

Sarah Pease of Salem Town, 1692

Arrested in May, accused of *sundry acts of Witchcraft*
committed on the bodys of Mary Warren, Abigaile Williams,
and Eliz Hubbard, she sat in a dungeon, her legs
in eight-pound chains. She must have wept when Bridget
Bishop and Rebecca Nurse returned, sentenced to be hanged.

She thought of the wool, shorn from neighbors' sheep,
that in an ordinary spring she'd wash and spin
for Robert to weave. Now he paid two shillings and five pence
per week for her prisoner's keep. In the garden their daughters
would be planting cabbage, turnips, rosemary and mint.

In her dreams the hangman's noose became a snake
wrapped around his own neck, and Reverend Noyes preached
the devil's word in the forest while the witches danced.
She helped Elizabeth Proctor give birth in the dungeon. Too bad
she couldn't conjure an earthquake, put the jailors in a trance.

By November the executions stopped, but Sarah stayed chained
until the governor pardoned all the accused in May.
Freed in time to plant pumpkins, potatoes and carrots,
she smiled at her spinning wheel, wooden dishes and iron pots
as sunlight sliced the windows and the clouds rose up in rage.

After the Battles

Benjamin Spooner, 1743-1827

Veteran of the French and Indian War,
at twenty Benjamin went back home
to his family's farm by Elder's Pond
in Middleboro, Massachusetts, wed
Mary Peirce and fathered seven children.

An on-call soldier, he answered the alarm
when Washington's army retreated
across the Delaware. He served bravely
eleven days, then went back home, took Mary
in his arms and fathered another child.

When the alarm sounded at Dartmouth
of course he went again, served two days,
then went back home. In 1780 he got
his final call, marched nine days, then went
back home and fathered two more children.

The year Mary died, he wed Tryphenia Booth,
seventeen years old, and fathered eleven more.
The second, Tryphenia Melinda, my great-
great-great-grandmother, loathed her name
and went by Melinda. Her kids numbered eight.

After the Gold Rush

Rowland Sturtevant Bumpus, 1804-1853

What father of ten working
at Tremont Nail Factory in Wareham,
Massachusetts, wouldn't buy
a steamship ticket to California
by way of Tierra del Fuego
with a stop in Panama, even
if the trip did take six months?

He envisioned gold everywhere
on the ground, gleaming under
redwoods, shining in every
stream, scattered amid fields
of poppies, and as easily picked.
He longed to give his wife Lucy
a mansion and luminous jewelry.

After months of hard work
and hunger, he found just enough
nuggets for his passage home,
went back to the factory until
he'd earned enough money
for another ticket, then tried again.
Who can blame a man for hope?

This time he came home coughing:
consumption. A forty-niner, he died
at forty-nine. Lucy buried him
at Agawam Cemetery with three
of their children. She'd miss his pay.
Nathan, their youngest, not yet six,
held her hand by the open grave.

In the Union Army

Nathan Cobb Bumpus, 1846-1926

That he ended up in a tent near Norfolk
in a four-button sack coat in December
was no one's doing but his own.
He'd joined the Massachusetts
Heavy Artillery, was assigned
to the 2nd Regiment, Company L,
which made him think of Lucy,
his mother, who'd begged him not to go,
but he was seventeen—old enough
to envision a world free of slavery
and hope for a role in creating it.
He'd read Lincoln's speech in November:
"a new nation, conceived in liberty,
and dedicated to the proposition
that all men are created equal." Now
he knew about amputees and the stench
of dead horses. Companies G and H
were captured by the Confederates
to a man. In the fall of '64, mosquitoes
carrying yellow fever descended
on Company B in New Bern, North
Carolina, bringing bleeding and seizures.
In April Company L replaced them.
Two months later the war was over.
Nathan mustered out in September
with enough ghosts and ailments to last
a lifetime. He headed home to Acushnet
where his mother lived on a farm
with her second husband, lovely Susan
Ellis was single, and my Grandpa Eben
and his siblings waited to be born.

Angenette Sampson

Dartmouth, Massachusetts, 1880

Thirty years old, live-in housekeeper,
she'd never wed or loved a man
and didn't think she ever would,
but that spring the Indian came
to plant parsnips, leeks and corn,
feed chickens, and milk the cows
on the Hazards' farm for a fraction
of a white man's wage. Her breath
quickened each day when he arrived.
She noticed his muscles, cheekbones,
long black braids, and he accepted
the coffee she brought to the barn.

The Wampanoags lived in shacks
by the pond outside of town.
She'd never been there but knew
the Indians were nearby and poor.
He brought her flowers, stones
and shells, said he was the *sachem*,
his people's leader. He loved her,
he said, but they couldn't go away.
She gave birth to a daughter
the following year, wouldn't tell
the father's name. The Hazards
fired him, but said she could stay.

Rachel Becomes Emma

Dartmouth, Massachusetts, 1892

Dirty snow covered the ground
and flocked the limbs of leafless trees
outside the window of the small, cold room
where Angenette coughed and wheezed.

Barely able to speak, she asked for Rachel,
her daughter, who helped her cook
and clean all day for the Hazards. The girl
stood at the foot of her mother's bed.

"Your father isn't dead," Angenette whispered.
"He watches you from the woods and leaves
gifts in the garden." She pointed to whelk
and periwinkle shells on the windowsill.

"He brought them here from the sea.
He knows the secrets of oaks and towhees.
If the Hazards ever mistreat you, go
to the Wampanoags. He's their chief."

She died the next day. Frederick and Mary
Hazard, who'd never had a child of their own,
told Rachel they would adopt her.
They called her Emma, her middle name,

and gave her the same warning
they'd given her mother: if she ever met
or mentioned the Indian, she couldn't enter
their house again. Like Angenette, she stayed.

The Family Secret

It started in Massachusetts, where pitch pine
grows with needles in bundles of three
and panic grass sways gracefully
at the edges of wetlands on Cape Cod.

The Hazards never wanted anything
revealed about the Indian—that disgrace—
but Emma told her daughter, my mother,
"Your grandfather was a Wampanoag chief."

My mother knew that nonnative plants
like Japanese honeysuckle and trumpet vine,
with its orange-red blossoms that drew
ruby-throated hummingbirds, grew there too.

In 1919, when the flu turned to pneumonia,
Emma coughed and wheezed. Like her mother
before her, she spat bloodstained mucus
on a winter morning and knew she would die.

Huckleberry and bearberry didn't yet
have any pink flowers, black oaks
and scrub oaks had no leaves, and no indigo
buntings or scarlet tanagers lit on the trees.

Emma's husband couldn't raise the children:
Ray, Fred, and my mother and Ethel, seven-
year-old twins. The Hazards brought the girls
to California and changed their last name,

but the twins never forgot the slurred whistle
of the northern cardinal, the small blue fruit
that robins plucked from red cedars, or the tale
of the lovers who met beneath these trees.

Uncle Fred

The farmhouse windows reflected
flames the night he set the barn on fire.
Nothing mattered but the hiss and roar.
Blue-hot fountains shot from the roof.

He'd lit a cigarette, let ashes fall
in the hayloft, felt satisfied when
the empty barn lit up the night. Still
a kid, he didn't care what happened.

His mother was dead, his father
working far away, his twin sisters
gone from him, his baby brother
boarding on a chicken farm upstate.

He knew the fire wouldn't bring
them back together, or do any other
good. The flames could be seen
all over Acushnet. That was enough.

The barn was saved, but even so,
his father's parents, who'd taken
him in, said yes when a couple
across town offered to adopt him.

I have a snapshot of him standing
in a driveway twenty years later,
his arms around my mom and aunt,
pipe dangling from his mouth,

the last time they saw him. He worked
in a shoe factory all his life, never

married, died at sixty and was buried
not far from his parents and the barn

he almost burned down. It collapsed
eighty years later, leaving just weeds
and the foundation. I've seen what
remains, known his anger and grief.

My Mother

I finally see what Dad saw in her—
not the apple-shaped woman
with full dentures at fifty
and a forties hairdo in 1962, not
the nag I scorned at fourteen

but a slim girl with firm breasts,
fabulous hats, and a new dress
for every occasion. He felt
he was dating a movie star.

She had dark hair and high cheekbones,
was part Wampanoag with hazel eyes
concealing who she was
and all her longings. She charmed him,
chatting easily about nothing.

She loved the World's Fair
on Treasure Island in 1939, laughed
at chipmunks, fed deer
from her hand at Yosemite,
and kissed my dad, he later said,
deeply and honestly.

I wish I could have been there
to see their joy before
he gambled away her inheritance
and her disappointments grew
round and hard, bitter fruit
that dropped to earth
and rotted, filled with seeds.

I Think of You When I'm Shopping

for clothes at Chic, sipping pink champagne
and nibbling chocolates. They trust me that much
as I try on alpaca sweaters from Peru and shirts
and pants hand-dyed with stripes and moons.
They know my name here, just as Tina
and Irene Sargent knew yours when you visited
the stores that carried their names. You liked
your shoes and purses to match, had your dresses
altered to be exactly the right number of inches
from the floor. Mrs. Brandes marked the hems
with chalk. I swung from the railing outside
the shop on Grand Avenue while you were fitted
for corsets. We don't wear those anymore,
thank God. You taught me to look for sales.
Today I'm getting thirty percent off. I'm sorry
I ever scorned you in your fox stole, the heads
draped around your shoulders, your pillbox hat
with velvet polka dots on its mesh veil,
and your necklace with all the little goldfish
embedded in plastic. I'd love to see you
again. I'll wear my pink linen pantsuit
from Belgium, my sandals from San Miguel,
and my necklace that looks like nested
luminous horseshoes when we meet
to find bargains in Pisces or the Pleiades.

Welcome Home

Welcome home to Mashpee
where snapping turtles and painted turtles bask
on logs in the marsh amid water willows,
ferns, and pickerel weed with purple flowers
reaching up from the shallows.

Welcome home to the place
where your great-grandfather whispered
to trout he caught at Santuit Pond,
then sat in a circle
and offered his pipe to Earth, Sky
and the Four Directions.

Welcome home to the coast
where your ancestors built *wetuash*
and gathered cranberries,
to the woods where they hunted
turkey, deer and bear,
and to the clearings clad
in goldenrods and asters
where they danced for 10,000 years.

Welcome home.
The elders have been waiting for you.
Listen to their drums, the beat
of your own heart.
Take this wampum necklace
made from the sacred shell
of the quahog clam.
When you wear it, walk through
redroot and wild lupine, hear
the quickening rhythm
of the field sparrow's song.

Instructions for a Wampanoag Clambake

Wade into Popponesset Bay
to collect some Rock People—
old round stones
smoothed by the tide.

Remember Moshup, the giant
who predicted the arrival of white men.
When he said good-bye
to the People of the First Light,

he turned into a whale.
Find a place in forest shade,
make a circle, and dig
a shallow round hole for the stones.

Moshup's friend, the giant frog,
came to the cliffs and wept.
Changed into a rock, he still sits
at Gay Head today and looks out to sea.

Before finding dry wood for the fire—
your gift from the forest—
notice the shape of the hole
and the stones: All life is a circle.

When the tide is low, gather
quahog and sickissuog clams
and plenty of rockweed,
whose stipes are loaded with brine.

Light a fire over the stones
and when the Rock People start to glow,

pile rockweed on them.
This is their blanket.

As saltwater is released
from the stipes and steam rises,
add clams, lobsters, corn,
more armfuls of rockweed.

This is the *apponaug:* seafood cooking.
Now thank Kehtannit, who saw
the frog's sorrow and turned
him into a rock out of pity

and taught the People to use
the Earth, plants, animals
and water to care for themselves
after Moshup left.

The deer will always make you laugh
the mountain lion take your side,
the Star People shine on your path
if you do it this way.

Business in DC

At thirty-three thousand feet
I think of my ancestors: the one
who yearned for his wife as he tended
the sick the first winter in Plymouth;
the one whipped at the post in 1645
for fornication; the ones who gathered
in the longhouse, wove bulrush mats
for floors of their *wetuash*, and taught
the Pilgrims how to plant maize.

What would they think of this view
of wrinkled hills, quilted farms
and glittering cities? Of cell phones,
email, fax machines and DVDs?
Would they be awed by ice-blue peaks
that rise from twisting river valleys?
Have fun Googling? Be shocked
by the war in Iraq, the Pacific
trash vortex and global warming?

I'd take my great-grandfather
who joined the Union Army in 1863
at seventeen to Ford's Theater to see
the single-shot pistol used to kill Lincoln,
the ones who fought the Redcoats
to see the Star-Spangled Banner
at the Smithsonian, its tattered wool
and cotton spread on a table where
conservators work behind glass.

At the Museum of the American Indian
I'd show all of them the baskets

whose designs mean people emerge
from previous worlds to enter this one.
I wish my forebears could gather in DC
for a stomp dance, then visit the National
Museum of Dentistry to contemplate ivory,
gold and asses' molars, all bound together,
in George Washington's false teeth.

Mythological Woman

I was born of the myths of Europe
and North America. My ancestors:
a Wampanoag chief who wore
necklaces of wampum and spoke
the languages of deer and salmon;
the passengers jammed in the cramped
and smelly hold of a cargo ship called
the *Mayflower* (they almost drowned
at sea, weren't ready for New England
weather, but lived to slip their DNA
to me); a baron whose castle glittered
on a hill above the Rhine (he rode
in gilded carriages, collected Greek
and Roman birdbaths until he lost
a battle with the king); a line of nobles
who lived in manors, blew their noses
with kings and queens, and served
as their advisors from Richard
the Lion Heart's Crusade until
the exodus to Massachusetts Bay.
None of this exempts me from the dishes.
I apply for jobs and get rejected, worry
about health insurance and taxes,
get stomachaches and corns, kvetch,
curse in anger, cough and sneeze.

Encounter With the Ancestors

A winter morning. Even before switching on the kitchen light, I see them in the dimness, sitting at the table, leaning against counters, standing at the sink—so many I can hardly squeeze my way through them: the Wampanoag chief and the white woman who bore his daughter; the nobleman who renounced the Church of England and received a one-way ticket to Massachusetts Bay; all the soldiers, farmers, ministers, and the women who fixed their dinners every night and kissed them on mornings like this as the dark began to fade; the teacher, the accountant, the miller, the milliner, the *Mayflower* passengers, the woman whipped at the post for adultery, the drunkard, the German baron who died in his fight against the king. A slender woman in a blue satin dress comes forward. "We've always been here," she says. "You just haven't noticed. We gave you your hazel eyes, high cheekbones and wavy hair; your stubbornness, love of chickadees and fondness for chocolate. Without us you'd be nothing but stardust—hydrogen, oxygen, carbon and iron from a couple of supernovae—now scattered on earth or zigzagging through the sea." A man in a green coat rises. "I'm from Plymouth," he says. "It isn't true we always wore black or gray. We liked bright colors. Our most common crime was fornication. Our drink of preference was beer." All at once they shout their demands: *Save the butterflies and whales! Do not blindly follow authority! Risk everything for love!* "It's too early in the morning for this," I protest. "Can't you come back after breakfast?" "Fight your battles to the end!" the baron proclaims, as I fill the French press pot with coffee and boiling water, just as I spot a hairy person with heavy brow ridges and big teeth on the back deck. I wonder what *he* wants. He points at the redwood tree. A squirrel scampers up the trunk, past a howler monkey hanging by its tail. Cells from the Precambrian sea wink all around me. I remember that soil is not wholly determined by bedrock and coffee is a shrub in the madder family. New universes bud from old. I press.

What We Missed

Atoms churning in the nothingness that was everything before planets congealed like cooling candy spheres; tectonic plates grinding against each other, then upthrusting to form mountains like hopes rising against all odds; the first cells to grow in colonies on rocks, unaware of their own shining; the sudden cluster of neurons (a brain!) in a flatworm on the floor of the sea; the stubby legs of the first awkward beings that stumbled onto land; the dinosaur egg that cracked open, releasing a leathery bird into the empty sky; the asteroid that smashed into Earth, filling the air with so much ash and dust that nearly everything died; the first shrewlike creature to suckle its young in a tree; the first hominid who used a stone as a tool to smash another stone; the slow journeys that took people from Africa to Europe, Asia and the Americas, one step at a time, through drought and snow; construction of the temples in Jerusalem, stone by pale stone. We missed the Ice Age, the Stone Age, the Bronze Age, the Iron Age, the Dark Ages, the Renaissance, the Industrial Revolution, the first staging of Hamlet, the *Mayflower's* arrival at Plymouth, Ben Franklin's kite, Edison's first lightbulb, the Wright brothers' flight. We missed it all—even our own births and all the moments of our lives—because we didn't go to the science center at Zilker Park. We stayed in our hotel room in Austin with the two double beds with gargantuan headboards and a view of cars and trucks, going somewhere, anywhere, rushing down I-35, leaving us behind.

Pneumonia

"It sounds like a washing machine,"
the pulmonologist says, stethoscope
to my chest. The CT scan shows
a meshwork of cobwebs
where alveoli should be clear.

Clots of mucus make my bronchi
appear bright white
in the image. Oh, dear!
With every breath I feel
and hear a rattle and wheeze.

Diagnosis: lobar pneumonia.
My mother's mother,
Emma Bumpus, thirty-seven
years old, mother of four, died
of lobar pneumonia in 1919.

And Emma's mother,
Angenette Sampson, died
of pneumonia in 1892,
the year Cleveland was re-elected,
before she turned forty-three.

I see the yellow mucus
from their chests each morning
and wake with them
in the middle of the night,
coughing, struggling to breathe.

Oh, to meet instead in a field
where winecup clarkia blooms

pink as a baby's lung
while dragonflies
zip through delicious air.

Blue Star and Yellow Moon

For Brandon

A blue star and a smiling yellow moon
dangle over a bassinette. The child
is transfixed. For him the world is new,
not a jigsaw of tectonic plates that quake
and grind, billions of years old. Too quickly
the shore erodes, as the heart falters.

Eventually even the stars will falter,
but for now the happy crescent moon
with a polka dot back turns quickly
when the mother reaches for the child
and bumps the star and moon, heart quaking
as she lifts her child, hungry, new.

The grandmother recalls when *she* was new,
before her sight began to falter,
before a lifetime lived in earthquake
country, before men walked on the moon.
She remembers the new mother as a child
sleeping in a bassinette. How quickly

she grew into a woman! How quickly
seed coats crack and life begins anew
with slim green shoots. All too soon the child
will see suffering. If he doesn't falter
perhaps someday he'll travel past the moon
or be the one to say why old stars quake.

Let each family member at the table quake
in amazement at the years that quickly

bloom, and smile like the child's moon
turning above the bassinette, brand new.
Let them catch each other if one falters
and not forget how stars look to a child.

I think the stars beam brightest for the child
too young to know the planet turns and quakes.
Taking his first step, the child will falter,
then pick himself up and try again quickly,
while his mother marvels at this new
thing to do beneath the sun and moon.

For now, the unfaltering little moon
is still, the child asleep beneath his new
star, light quaking as the Earth turns quickly.

Becoming an Ancestor

According to the dictionary, I'm not
an ancestor yet, only a grandparent
of a blond boy who clomps in his new sandals,
then throws me a ball strewn with black
stars and moons on a white background,
and a bow-legged baby girl with blue eyes,
all smiles today in her hooded carrier—
a child born the day my own grandfather
would have turned 130. He never knew
he had grandchildren, let alone great greats.

My own toddler days of warm cookies,
crayons and Betsy Wetsy dolls don't seem
far away, but I am en route to becoming
an ancestor. Lucy and Ricky are dead.
Barbie is past fifty. Even the hippies
are history. When my grandchildren show
their grandchildren my photo in an old
album, I wonder what they'll say.
That I swore like a trucker when I was hurt?
Blew like Vesuvius when I was mad?

They might recall I was always late, never
learned to knit or crochet, had brown hair,
couldn't cook worth a damn but could carry
a tune, took poetry books everywhere,
liked to know birds and insects by name,
overreacted in both bad and good ways,
was unreasonably vain for someone my age,
had legs like a crane and liked to dance.

Children at Play

The boy hits his sister, who sits next to him
on the sofa. He's eight. She's six.
She hits him back. He pushes her.
She pushes him. They're both laughing.

Should I put a stop to this? She kicks him,
and he grabs her in a chokehold.
Grandpa says, "Stop! That could hurt her."
He shoves her face into the sofa. "Stop!"

When he lets go, she stands and he pushes
her into the coffee table. She starts to cry.
Their parents left five minutes ago.
They're ours for five more hours.

Taking her in my arms, I tell him to apologize.
I should have stopped them after
that first smack. He runs off as I comfort her.
The bedroom door slams, then the back door.

She goes after him. He's barricaded himself
in the unfinished addition to the house,
won't speak to anyone. Grandpa says,
"Leave him alone. He feels guilty."

Will we make it to pizza and the movie?
Yes. Sullen, back inside, he snarls, "Sorry."
"He always says it like that," she says.
His hands cover his ears in the car.

At the food court, he's ready to talk,
asks for pepperoni pizza. Now he's okay.
My thoughts drift to instincts and caves.
Saber-toothed tigers. He'll protect me someday.

Boy at Pinball

For Brandon

Blond and brown-eyed, almost nine,
he leans in and tries to hit the flipper
just in time to shoot the ball back
over the waves to the SeaWitch's face
amid the clinks and bells of dozens
of machines lined up at the Pinball Museum.

He's interested but not swept away
by these antiques. The game lacks
the complications of Pokémon, the thrill
of a Skylanders battle, the smack
of a soccer ball, but he braves it long
enough to rack up points on the backbox.

His grandfather, slender and seventeen,
played avidly at Rosie's Diner
while I sat on a round red stool as he
pulled the plunger and steel balls zipped
through the maze, "Poison Ivy" blasting
on the jukebox. He always won a replay.

The boy tries other machines. Red
and green pop bumpers light up
as the ball bounces off them. Bells ring,
points scored. He takes aim but misses
the gobble hole, and the ball careens toward
the drain. Gone, like all teenage dreams.

Names of the Horses

For Sabine at six

I want to remember the names
you gave the little plastic horses—
the females Sandy and Buttercup,
the males Lightning and Gray—
and how they ran in pairs through
the canyons and mountains of the house,
two in your small hands, your hair
pulled back in a long blond braid,
two in my own grandmotherly hands,
following close behind on the trails
that led to the alpine meadows
of the upstairs bedrooms, then down
to the valley where they bathed
in a stream rushing through the playroom
in the basement. Back upstairs at the ranch
in the living room, they ate hay, and I
watched as you lovingly bathed them
again and gave them new shoes, each
in his or her turn, before they took off
for another expedition through the wilds
of the house, and when they reached
that stream in the basement again,
I spread a blanket on the sandy shore
and lay back, exhausted, to watch you play.

Autumn, the Girl

Autumn Rose makes hoopoes whoop in me.
Daughter of my daughter, four years old,
she draws fairies and writes poetry
about the queen of water. She told
us this kind monarch also rules the day.
In cartoons she scorns mean clouds and monsters
who snarl or roar, preferring bears who play
fair with friends and mice who become dancers.

Yet she speaks knowingly of pterodactyls
and getting good jobs with an MBA.
She doesn't shy away from things like fractals
at the science center high above the bay,
which shines like metal as the sun goes down
and she proclaims, "The queen has on her crown!"

Devlin at Seven Months
and the Morning News

Mubarak resigns while you crawl
toward the yellow plastic castle
with the red door, the little king,
queen and knight perched on top.

Brightly colored shapes and letters—
triangle, circle, hexagon, square,
A, B, C, D—are scattered on the rug
for you to gather and examine.

This is more important today
than the 500-year-old grapevine
destroyed by vandals in Austria,
or even the opposition leader placed

under house arrest in Tehran.
Come spin the tiny drum, slide
the colored rings, and press
the squeaky button just for fun.

Let's not worry about the UFO
that hovered over the Dome
of the Rock, then shot into the sky,
or the man who hit a woman

with a stone on a cruise ship near
the island of Cozumel before
throwing her body into the sea.
My grandson, keep banging

the castle with the triangle; smile
your wide smile. We can save
the world some other day.
For now, just reach for the B.

Naturalists

For Devlin

Two years old, he takes my hand,
leads me to the blackberry vine
growing on the fence in his backyard.

They're not ripe yet, he explains,
then points to a small hole
in the earth. *The ants live there.*

I need a digging stick, he announces,
holding up a fragile twig and shaking
his head. *This one's no good.*

I hand him a thicker stick. *Perfect!*
In a shady corner near the patio
he digs and makes a find.

It's a roly-poly in a ball, he says.
I hold out my hand to receive
the woodlouse, a terrestrial crustacean.

Gretchen and I called them pill bugs
in first grade when we found them
with ants and Jerusalem crickets.

Careful! My grandson warns.
A pincer bug! It will pinch you.
He points to an earwig, an insect

with cerci: forceps on its abdomen.
It's had five molts before
becoming an adult. Someday

I will tell him this, and that females
have straight pincers, males curved ones.
Today, though, he's the teacher,

and I'm his eager pupil, standing
in light while blackberries ripen
and a woodlouse unrolls.

Returning to The Butchart Gardens

Fifty years ago, rushing ahead of my parents
and friend Sharon, I ran down these same paths
edged with lobelias and blue poppies
on Vancouver Island. Sea hollies bobbed
like small purple pinecones on stalks, canna lilies
waved pink silks, begonias danced in several shades
of red. The Sunken Garden, once a limestone quarry,
overflowed with dahlias and hydrangeas. I'd never
been in an airplane; no one had a cell phone
or computer; no one had walked on the moon.

What have I done these fifty years? Fell in love
with a field of wild irises and a boy I met
at Al's Drive-In when I was fourteen, wore
a tight, blue-satin Chinese dress to our wedding
seven months later, bore a daughter while pink
and lavender mariposa tulips opened, left
my husband, stapled lids to chicken dinner plates
for a living, missing the blue-runner violet's
spectacular display, married the same man
again at seventeen, while slender sunflowers
nodded their yellow heads in an autumn breeze,
left him again in spring, when fire poppies ignited
the coastal range, learned to solve differential
equations and identify the parts of a flower
(pistil, stigma, style, ovary, anther, filament),
fell in love with a man who said at a party,
"You look like you want to dance," married
him in a meadow by a redwood grove
where chickweed looked like drifts of snow,
bore another daughter, measured the electrical

68

potential across the membrane of an egg cell
of a mud whelk, wrote technical manuals,
left my husband, taught students to distinguish
between monocots and dicots by the veins
in their leaves, interviewed scientists, wrote about
how the universe bloomed from a single seed,
ran a health museum, wrote poems filled
with wildflowers, fell in love again, married
him under a canopy whose poles were twined
with pink, red, white and yellow roses, held
bronze urns containing my parents' ashes
on a hillside above the bay, read *Bambi*, played
Candy Land, and watched *Cinderella* and *Dumbo*
with my grandchildren while seasons changed
and the rhododendrons in my front yard grew
heavy again with bell-shaped flowers.

Of course, Mrs. Butchart's gardens look different
now, smaller, the roses no longer in bloom.
Arched trellises, once laden with red blossoms
hanging over the path, are wound with empty vines.
I reach the end, the Italian Garden—so genteel
with its walkways and cross-shaped central bed
of marigolds and peonies—just before the gift shop.
But I want to go back, so I run to the head
of the path and make a mad dash, sprinting now
back toward the Sunken Garden for one more look
before the delphiniums and begonias fade.

Delinquent Sonnets

In Juvenile Hall
New Juvie has bright paintings on the walls
to celebrate the better things in life:
nature, growth, transformation. These murals
admonish, "Graduate! Put down your knife."
Mustard-colored cells are stacked in tiers,
windowless, with built-in cots and stools,
where teenagers, alone, confront their fears
and contemplate new ways to break the rules.

The year I was thirteen I ran away
from home and landed here. Back then my cell
had a window. I could watch grass sway
on a hillside, hear jays and warblers call.
More pleasing than a work of art to me:
a glimpse of sky, a hummingbird, a bee.

Wild Kid
I finally have become the proper girl
my mother always wanted me to be.
I don't smoke hash or grass, wear mini-skirts,
pick up long-haired, tattooed men or party
till the neighbors call the police. My last
drunken binge was nineteen seventy.
My motorcycle-riding days are past.
I haven't shoplifted since sixty-three.

Oh, Mama, what's to become of me?
I've no regrets for anything I did—
the mescaline, the baby at fifteen.
Inside, I'll always be your wild kid.
I'd gladly wear those mini-skirts again
if I had the legs I did back then.

The Girl I Never Was

The girl I never was didn't start
smoking when she was twelve.
She was meticulous about
her school uniform and learned
to speak French in seventh grade.

She didn't drop out of school
or have a baby at fifteen. God no!
She was a cheerleader in high school
and valedictorian. Every college
she applied to offered a scholarship.

And now she is angry with me
about the life she didn't lead.
"You ruined it all!" she complains.
She never even got to attend a prom,
she says. How could I do this to her?

She has grown into a nonexistent
woman who nevertheless nags me.
Why didn't you let me learn
to cook sea bass with cress purée
perfectly, or be a Girl Scout leader?

She says she wanted to spend more
time than I did with my aging parents
and my children when they were small.
Couldn't I just have let her take them
to Fairyland a little more often?

What can I say? If I'd indulged her,
well, my children wouldn't exist. I know
she's the better person, but she wants
me to be the nonentity. I tell her
I'm sorry. Am I? Only she can say.

I Remember

Red machines that dispensed
nickel Cokes in glass bottles
when my dad filled his '55 Olds

Leaving our order for the milkman
using tags that stuck out
of a bottle on the back porch

Begging my dad to trade in
the blue-and-white Olds
for a '57 Chevy Bel Air with fins

Being warned to stay away
from the round washing machine
with the external wringer

Always getting tagged by Karen
when we played kick the can
in the middle of the street

The red plastic hula hoop
I twirled on my skinny hips
longer than my cousin Jan

The purple print and sweet scent
of mimeographed math drill sheets
that Mrs. O'Gara handed out

My keen disappointment
when air raid drills were discontinued:
no more ducking under desks

The Mickens' black dog Lucky
running through the neighborhood
and pooping on the sidewalk

Having a crush on Elvis Presley
and buying "Love Me Tender"
on a 78-rpm record

The doctors who came to my house
and pulled thermometers
and shots from their black bags

Playing with the X-ray machine
that showed the outline of my shoes
and the bones of my feet in green

Ratting my hair on top
into a four-inch dome and gluing
it in place with hairspray

Making out at drive-ins
while incredibly boring
black-and-white movies played

Girls who liked sex being
called nymphomaniacs and girls
who refused being called frigid

Police dogs attacking
and fire hoses spraying
people who wanted equal rights

Using a slide rule and being told
a girl could never be
as good as a boy at math

Being told that girls only
go to college to find a husband
and should always let the boys win

Deciding to beat the boys at math
drink beer smoke grass and take on
the lies in my gold lamé pants

San Francisco East Bay Houses

The one near Grand Avenue in "lower" Piedmont,
where my mother had cared for her grandparents
and I hated being an only child

The one where I lived with my aunt, uncle
and cousin in Oakland, so I wouldn't
have to go to Piedmont Junior High

The cottage where I stayed with my boyfriend
and his grandmother in Oakland
after my aunt and uncle evicted me

The mouse-infested Victorian apartment
near downtown Oakland that we moved into
after our wedding when I was fourteen

The mouse-infested, massive pink stucco
apartment complex in Concord,
where we partied until my husband lost his job

My parents' house again, where I arranged
my stuffed animals on the headboard
of the bed where my husband and I slept

The studio apartment in Oakland
with the Murphy bed, where I lived
with my daughter after the divorce

The rear cottage we rented in Oakland
when I married the same man again,
only to leave him five months later

The apartment near Lake Merritt,
where I stayed only a few nights
because a man I feared knew the address

The apartment on Oakland Avenue,
another pink stucco building,
where I lived when I finished high school

The triplex on Montgomery Street
in Oakland, where I was bitten
on the ankle by a German shepherd

The apartment in University Village
in Albany, where my seven-year-old daughter
stood in a stairwell and screamed when I was late

Another apartment in University Village,
where I slept on a mattress on the floor
and hung rock posters and a beaded curtain

A third apartment in University Village,
where my daughter had a white rat
and cockroaches convened under the cage

The neoclassic row house beside a creek
in Oakland, where I fought with another husband
and my second daughter was born

The rambling old house in Oakland
with lots of woodwork, just a few blocks
from the first one in Piedmont

The condo in Berkeley where I lived for a year
with my third husband, and we watched
the sun set behind the Golden Gate

The rambling house in Oakland
we returned to, where I dream of my parents,
other husbands, my daughters as children

and sometimes wake wondering where I am,
what the dead are trying to tell me, what I did
with my ticket, and which way is home

Melanoma

Small black mole on top
of a large brown one
on my leg, it could be
a beauty mark but is more
like a black hole, ready
to claim all the days
of my past and future:
childhood afternoons
at the playground,
swinging and sliding
in shorts and sleeveless
little blouses; my teens
when I lay on the grass,
a sacrifice to the sun;
my twenties when I wore
a pink bikini to study
outdoors amid poppies
holding out their gleaming
orange bowls. A pity
I was never a swimmer
or tennis player, at least
strengthening my body
while I steeped in
ultraviolet radiation.
I was just a foolish
woman who wanted
to be more beautiful.
Now the mole must be
cut away from my flesh,
leaving a hole in my leg,
before it sucks in

everything—future
nights and afternoons,
friends, family, dreams,
planets, moons—
beneath its dark horizon.

The Lost Necklaces

Searching through drawers
and jewelry boxes, unable
to find it, anxiety rising,
I tell my husband: I can't
find the iridescent necklace
you gave me. Do you
remember it? Did I dream
or imagine it? He can't
recall an iridescent necklace
but wants to know what
I did with the necklace
from Mexico he gave me
last year. It was very
expensive. I don't remember
a necklace from Mexico.
He doesn't remember
what it looked like.
Two missing necklaces!
I feel awful. How
it must hurt him—I've lost
two necklaces he gave me
and can't even remember
one of them. Frantic,
back upstairs, I look
again through drawers,
find a red box, in it
an iridescent necklace.
He says it's Mexican opal
set in silver. I didn't remember
it was from Mexico.
He didn't remember

it was iridescent. There
are no lost necklaces.
We are only losing
our minds.

The Lost Books

What happened to the books I thought would be
in neat rows in my library forever,
dear old friends who'd rush to comfort me

whenever I was bored or sick or lonely
or vexed by things I wanted to remember?
What happened to the books I thought would be

dependable as stars that come out nightly
and take their places in the Bull or Hunter,
dear old friends who'd always shine on me

as clouds dispersed and I sipped ginger tea?
Why didn't they tell me it was over?
Where did they go, the books I knew would be

my pals until the end? How did they leave?
En masse? In groups of two or three, no longer
dear old friends with any use for me?

Perhaps I should have come more frequently,
assured them that I cared, just like a lover.
What happened to the books I came to need
like dear old friends one doesn't often see?

I Am Afraid

I am afraid I will write a masterpiece
and people will mistake it
for an old pot.
I am afraid I will write and write
all day for years, and the pot
will remain empty.
I am afraid I will have no time
to fill the pot
let alone write a masterpiece.

I am afraid I will go to sleep booing
like a screech owl
into my yellow pillowcase
and wake up still booing
like a screech owl.
I am afraid I will never stop booing
and my pillow will get moldy
and my husband will get mad.

I am afraid I will make a mistake,
erase it,
then make the same mistake
over and over again.
I am afraid the erasure dust
will make me sneeze.

I am afraid people will give me
only dogbane and thorns,
never invite me into their gardens,
turn away my offerings
of sage and thyme.

I want to go to Mars, Venus, Jupiter,
where no one knows me,
where no one can see
my old pot,
my soggy pillowcase,
my erasures,
my scratched hands.

I am afraid there are no more tickets
to Mars, Venus or Jupiter.

I am afraid I will wake
some morning, eat breakfast
and not remember
my breakfast.
I am afraid I will mistake an egg
for a masterpiece. I am afraid
I won't live long enough
to forget I ate breakfast
and the difference between
a masterpiece and an empty old pot.

Medical Test

After I guzzle 48 ounces of water
in one and one-half hours,
my bladder is ready to burst,

but the ultrasound technician is pleased
that this swollen organ presses
my intestines out of the way.

She examines my uterus, tubes
and ovaries, which look like a field
of gravel on the display—quite

a moonscape, with no interesting
geologic features like the San Andreas,
Mount McKinley or Half Dome.

This is such good news, I could
be an astronaut or dance like Isadora.
Surely there must be more in store

for me this afternoon than checking
my post office box and stopping
by the drugstore for vitamins. I want

to grab the hand of the universe
and spin like a galaxy with no
black holes, stars streaming into space.

Late Apologies to Betsy

I can't find the prints you gave me
as a wedding gift in 1974.
They hung in my dining room for thirteen years,
but that marriage ended, and then I moved.

The drawings were lovely.
The abstract ones looked like Oriental
calligraphy, and I smiled every time I passed
"Fish Rubbing Himself on Man with Beer."

They were in an upstairs closet I cleaned out
eight years ago. I've never lost
a friend's artwork before,
but that was the year my dad died

and my third husband moved in.
We sent truckloads of things to Goodwill.
I enjoyed the time you visited me at work.
The idea of a walk in Tilden Park sounded good.

I don't know why I didn't follow through
either then or when we talked about
going to a vegetarian restaurant for lunch
or dinner with our men.

The note about your book, *Morning in Saramatu*,
is still in a pile of things on my desk.
I always meant to pick it up
from the poetry table at Black Oak.

When did they go out of business?
When did I grow too lazy to call

friends who don't use email? How many years
has it been since we laughed over cheese and bread?

When did you stop being
a young woman with long honey-colored hair?
I would have liked to see you again
and laugh some more. That much is clear.

Elegant Toe

Death wears a black tuxedo
—Zvi A. Sesling

Death wears a red satin dress
with sequins and ruffles,
silver shoes, a ruby ring,
a red camellia in her hair.

With polka-dot nail polish
on fingers and toes, she points
an elegant toe toward the great
chartreuse unknown.

She smiles beguilingly,
revealing perfect teeth,
drinks Margaritas
with salt on the glass.

Her red is the red
of beginnings, of walking
red pathways, searching
for a hidden wall—

the one beyond which
everything you ever wanted lies,
the one that is high and slippery,
impossible to climb.

Letting Go

When you jump with a parachute,
everything tiny and far away,
when you leave your childhood,
when you slide from the turntable
in the funhouse, you have no control.
Letting go of your dreams
you feel lighter, careening
toward some other destination.
You must let go of your children
(they were never really yours)
and your life, that uncomfortable suit,
a little too tight, with the odd
pattern you never could figure out,
the fabric slowly becoming light and rain.

Again

After a long night of rain
I drove west, over a bridge
heading into clouds
fluffed on the horizon.

The bay, dotted with rocky
islands, rippled sweetly,
but bitter things now drip
into the arm of the woman

getting chemo: Rituxan,
a clear liquid that kills b cells,
Cytoxan, Doxorubicin,
Vincristine from periwinkles.

Her IV pole has six legs—
an insect, strange and round,
with an immense chrome
proboscis rising from its back.

Blue nitrile gloves poke
from boxes behind the bed
where the woman sleeps, a cap
on her head, her body wrapped

in a blanket like the day
she was born, when the nurse
placed her in my arms, a six-
pound, eleven-ounce bundle.

Snoring softly, she stirs,
perhaps dreaming. Soon
she will wake, and again
I will take her home.

ICU

In your blue hospital gown
you are at peace here,
attached to a machine that eases
your breathing. It sends you
a pulse of air every few seconds.

A tangle of tubes and IV lines
delivers fentanyl citrate,
dexamethasone, dextrose,
electrolytes and protein.

On the black monitor screen
your pulse shows up
in green at 113 beats per minute,
oxygen saturation in aqua,
100 percent. Your 12 breaths
per minute appear in white,
blood pressure readings in pink.

All this is good. Your cheeks rosy
as you sleep. Tomorrow,
my daughter, they will take you back
to radiation. For now, I am relieved

to see you swaddled in sheets,
still breathing. May you dream
of mountain fields
and crescent-shaped beaches,
the sea shimmering behind you
as you as run across the sand,
sunlight like liquid on your shoulders.

Breathe deep; the air is clean.

Bone Marrow Donor

I want to give life again, the way
the redwood tree outside my window
makes new pale needles at the ends
of branches turning brown,

the way the rhododendrons
in my front yard shout pink
and purple again in the sunlight
caressing them each spring,

the way my belly grew round
with baby daughters kicking
and writhing inside, so long ago.
Now one of them is dying.

May stem cells from my marrow
bloom for her, that she might
make white cells free of cancer
and I can give her life one more time.

Live!

For Liana

Live
to see fields of California poppies
glow again—four-petaled,
shining orange corollas
like silky flames floating
on long stems above
a lacework sea of bluish leaves.

Live
to hear trees buzz with cicadas
contracting and relaxing
their tymbal muscles in summer
while barn swallows with
dark wings and rusty breasts
croon long, twittering songs.

Live
to taste aged cheddar
and French bread on the trail
while Steller's jays strut,
their punky feather crests jutting
upward, and Oregon juncos,
black-hooded, savor bugs.

Live
to touch the buttercup's
yellow satin, the checkerbloom's
smooth stem and hairy leaves,
the sticky monkey flower's resin,
the cobweb thistle's spines
and red petals, toothpick-thin.

Live
to sniff bay laurel leaves
broken in your palm,
their sharp, oily perfume filling
your nose, and brush against
coyote mint, its leaves
releasing their sweetness.

And if you can't live any longer
in your beautiful body
made of stardust, sonatas and rain,
then live in the sighs and easy
smiles of your children,
the muscular rooms of

our hearts, and the clusters
of treelike cells in our brains
where the moments of your life
return like the poppies'
small fires to light up
bleak fields again and again.

Rituals

A sunflower thrown on the water at dusk
the day you died.
I stood on the bluff to watch
it float away.

Poems, a photo, a bell and a rose
placed beside a bronze urn
in a vault to be covered
with flowers and dirt.

Small mementoes and photos of you
sewn inside stuffed toys:
a bear your son named Captain Puffy,
a cat your daughter named Katy.

A stake bearing your name
driven into the earth
beneath a redwood
whose upper branches wave and wave.

A future of fat white candles
to be lit for you each year.
Yit-gadal v'yit-kadash sh'may raba...
May there be abundant peace...Amen.

If I Had to Write a Poem

I would say the sky is low and gray today,
an immense stone pressing on the Bay Area,
matching the one inside me, its weight
pulling me down while all the bridges
dissolve in mist and traffic on Highway 80
inches along. It seems so wrong that the world
goes on without you, my daughter, vowing
to kick cancer's butt, the way you once vowed
to quit your addiction to bad boyfriends, and did.

Sweet girl, I know now that you wanted me,
not your stepfather, to carry you at night
from the car to the house when you were eight,
not because you hated him but because you
needed me to hold you. Oh, how I wished
I could, but you were too heavy, even then.

When I Can't Sleep

In my darkened room I listen
to faraway trains calling
like forlorn birds and the murmur
of distant traffic, which sounds
like the sea, and think about
my daughter Liana, how I didn't
believe she was dying. What good
did that do? She believed, too,
that she could beat the cancer,
but the odds were against her
and the magic never came through.
Her name, carved and painted
white, looked out of place on
the headstone amid all the ones
that had weathered away. I had
the others repainted—those of
my parents and my mother's
grandparents—as though this
assured they were keeping her
company, that she would
not be alone for eternity
and both of us could sleep.

Voyage of Life

After four paintings by Thomas Cole

Childhood
My boat glided in calm water, warmth
radiating from the angel who stood
close behind me, hand on the tiller
as we drifted past waxy lotuses

and banks overhung with ferns and roses.
A winged golden figure on the prow
held an hourglass filled with sand
just beginning to fall. I couldn't see

the barren crags in the distance.
My mother, with shining brown hair,
waved from the shore, and my father
snapped pictures as I laughed and clapped.

Youth
I held the tiller myself as the boat
drifted toward a castle on the horizon,
mine for the finding. No one told me
it was a mirage or pointed out the bend

in the stream. Perhaps my parents
believed in it too. At least the lilies, oaks
and elms were real. The angel watched
from under a palm on the bank.

I examined the branching of leaf veins
and marveled at the purple of irises.
The sky was blue, serene as the water,
which mirrored the trees as sand fell and fell.

Adulthood
I couldn't believe where I had come to:
a place of crags and rapids, trees
gnarled, shattered, nearly leafless.
The tiller broke off; the hours themselves

shook with fear. Need I mention the sky
clotted with clouds, rain drenching
barren earth, the hourglass half empty?
The angel had withdrawn from my side.

I was far past the point where my parents
could help, though surely they'd want to.
Alone with my dreams and skimpy clothing,
I kept my eyes open and sped downstream.

Old Age
I haven't reached the end, but glimpsed it
when my parents got there. My daughter
passed me, arrived there without growing old.
The water was still, the hourglass missing,

the great figure gone from the prow.
The rocks held no vegetation. Perhaps
the angel was near, but I couldn't see her.
Unable to help, I watched from a distance,

wanting the last breaths to be easy. I hope
they were so. Now my grandchildren
ride the boat laden with flowers. I name
the star tulips, share small things I know.

Yom Kippur

Kol Nidre
A symphony—the long
melodious chant of swallows
that rise sunward, beating
like a thousand hearts.
They sing of the wound
and blood's dark tendrils,
of the hidden nest
and the slow healing.
They land in a field
of blue flowers
as darkness unfolds
and cold stars settle.

Torah
Two goats. One
is to be sacrified:
straight bones and firm
muscles will burn.
The other receives the sins
of the people, goes free.
The burden twists him;
skin and muscles rip.
He wanders alone, blind,
edging into dusk.

Ne'ilah
Again the day rolls
into darkness; the sky
spills its pinks and purples,
draining to blackness. Deep

inside there is a closing,
a small gate
swinging shut in the mind.
Those few last thoughts
rush through, and a life
is sealed. Outside the temple
a lone bird sounds its call,
waits for response.

Essay on Time

Time fills a horned lark
singing its riff of high-pitched notes
by a field of silver hairgrass
whose spikelets shine
like bright metal on a winter morning.

It's the telomeres at the ends
of chromosomes, shrinking with each
division of every cell
of the hairgrass and lark
until the cells can't divide.

It's the San Andreas,
a strike-slip fault deep beneath
the field, stretched out
like a serpent that will rouse
to gulp down hairgrass and houses.

It's also the sun, whose light
falls evenly on the field,
a yellow dwarf star
that someday will become
a red giant, boiling away Earth's water.

What is time but the universe,
a self-creating vacuum
studded with suns and planets
that sweep in their orbits
like the hands of billions of clocks?

Time flies, divides, trembles, burns,
arises from and returns

to nothing. It holds the dead tight
while the lark sings this morning
and stars blink out.

When I Die

Let the sky be blue as a Steller's jay
and rippled with clouds, the trail
be rimmed with blossoms blowing
in wind soft as baby's breath.
Notice the red maids, each with five
bright petals and hairy-edged sepals,
and sun cups—light-filled chalices
on stalks ringed with oval leaves.

Take a lance-like leaf from a bay tree,
break it and breathe deeply. Look
for the black cap and yellow breast
of a Wilson's warbler if you hear
a series of musical chirps, dropping
slightly in pitch toward the end,
coming from the willow by the stream.

*

Wear vermilion, indigo or violet. Eat
wild mushroom risotto with fresh thyme
and Taleggio cheese. Take a bite
of curried chicken with eggplant relish.
Let your tongue caress fresh
strawberries, kiwi fruit and grapes.

Taste—no, devour!—the chocolate-hazelnut
truffle tart. Open a bottle of chardonnay.
Read a poem that mentions luminous cells
or blue-pod lupine, its curved banner petals
waving on a cliff by the raucous sea.

*

Put on a CD that's good for dancing,
maybe rock'n'roll from the fifties or sixties.
I always liked Little Richard and the Beatles.
Move as the music enters your body. Feel
your heart beat faster, then think of me.

I will be your partner, the air and light
that surround you. Give yourself
to the rhythm as arms and legs lead you.
I will be there, spinning with you.
Trust me. I won't step on your feet.

Acknowledgments

I am grateful to my husband, Richard Michael Levine, and to my many poet friends for helping me improve these poems. I am also grateful to the editors of the following publications, in which some of the poems have appeared, sometimes in slightly different form:

Anthropology and Humanism: "I Always Knew It"

Arroyo Literary Review: "Delinquent Sonnets"

Berkeley Poetry Review: "Essay on Time," "My Mother"

Berkeley Poets Cooperative: "Letting Go"

Blue Lyra Review: "I Am Afraid," "Rituals"

Blue Unicorn: "After the Battles," "Elizabeth Contemplates Her Will," "John and Sarah Bumpus, 1692" "My Grandmother's Painting"

Blue Violin: "Disneyland, 1956"

California Quarterly: "Bone Marrow Donor," "If I Had to Write a Poem," "Uncle Fred"

Catamaran Literary Reader: "Live!"

The Cincinnati Review: "The Lost Books"

Crack the Spine: "Pneumonia"

ForPoetry.com: "Becoming an Ancestor," "Business in DC," "Return to Acushnet"

FRiGGmagazine.com: "Elegant Toe"

The Great American Poetry Show: "In the Union Army"

Haight Ashbury Literary Review: "San Francisco East Bay Houses"

The Hudson Review: "Figurines," "The Lost Necklaces," "Naturalists"

Iodine Poetry Journal: "I Think of You When I'm Shopping"

ISLE: Interdisciplinary Studies in Literature and Environment: "Clouds"

Jewish Women's Literary Annual: "Melanoma"

LevureLitteraire.com: "Blue Star and Yellow Moon," "Children at Play," "Names of the Horses"

The MacGuffin: "Angenette Sampson," "Rachel Becomes Emma"

Marin Poetry Center Anthology: "ICU"

Miramar: "Again"

Naugatuck River Review: "When I Can't Sleep"
North Coast Literary Review: "The Girl I Never Was," "Mythological Woman"
Passager: "Aunt Ethel, Please"
Paterson Literary Review: "Devlin at Seven Months and the Morning News"
Poemeleon.org: "Encounter with the Ancestors," "What We Missed"
PoetryMagazine.com: "Voyage of Life"
Poetry Now: "Medical Test"
Psychological Perspectives: "Glass Animals"
Quercus Review: "When I Die"
QuillandParchment.com: "Dad and the Gypsy"
Redactions: "Journeys," "Puzzle"
Schuylkill Valley Journal: "My Mother's Mixer"
TowerJournal.com: "The Family Secret," "Instructions for a Wampanoag Clambake," "Welcome Home"
Turning a Train of Thought Upside Down: An Anthology of Women's Poetry (Scarlet Tanager): "Returning to The Butchart Gardens"
Valparaiso Poetry Review: "Autumn, the Girl"
Voices Within the Ark: The Modern Jewish Poets (Avon): "Yom Kippur"
Wild Goose Poetry Review: "Edward and Hannah Bumpus" (as "My Mother's Roots"), "Pilgrimage," "Sarah Pease of Salem Town, 1692"
Women's Words of Wisdom (Blue Mountain Press): "Great-Grandmother"

"Aunt Ethel, Please" received Honorable Mention in the 2006 *Passager* Poetry Contest and the 2007 Jewel by the Bay Poetry Contest, and was reprinted in *Burning Bright: Passager Celebrates 21 Years* (Passager Books). "Devlin at Seven Months and the Morning News" received Honorable Mention in the 2014 Allen Ginsberg Poetry Awards and was reprinted in the *Marin Poetry Center Anthology*. "Edward and Hannah Bumpus," "Angenette Sampson," "Rachel Becomes Emma," and "The Family Secret" were reprinted in *The Great American Poetry Show*. "I Always Knew It" received Honorable Mention in the 2006 Society for Humanistic Anthropology Poetry Contest. "Instructions for a Wampanoag Clambake" was reprinted in the Poem-Pairs Blog. "Journeys" was nominated for a Pushcart Prize and reprinted in *New California Writing 2012* (Heyday). "Pilgrimage" was reprinted in *QuillandParchment.com*. "Rituals" received a Best of the Net nomination. "Welcome Home" received Honorable Mention in the 2013 Janice Farrell Poetry Prize category of the Soul-Making Keats Literary Competition. "Yom Kippur" was reprinted in *From the Well of Living Waters* (Kehilla Community Synagogue). "Ne'ilah," from "Yom Kippur," has been reprinted many times in the annual *Central Synagogue Memory Book* (Central Synagogue of New York).

The following poems appeared in previous books by Lucille Lang Day: "Letting Go" and "Yom Kippur" in *Self-Portrait with Hand Microscope*; "Great-Grandmother" in *Wild One*; "Boy at Pinball," "Business in DC," and "What We Missed" in *Dreaming of Sunflowers: Museum Poems*.

About the Author

Lucille Lang Day is the author of nine previous poetry collections and chapbooks, including *The Curvature of Blue*, *The Book of Answers*, and *Infinities*. Her first poetry collection, *Self-Portrait with Hand Microscope*, received the Joseph Henry Jackson Award in Literature; her most recent chapbook, *Dreaming of Sunflowers: Museum Poems*, won the Blue Light Poetry Award. She has also published a children's book, *Chain Letter*, and a memoir, *Married at Fourteen: A True Story*, which received a PEN Oakland Josephine Miles Literary Award and was a finalist for the Northern California Book Award in Creative Nonfiction. Day earned her M.F.A. in creative writing at San Francisco State University and her Ph.D. in science/mathematics education at the University of California at Berkeley. The founder and director of a small press, Scarlet Tanager Books, she also served for seventeen years as the director of the Hall of Health, an interactive museum in Berkeley. She lives in Oakland, California, with her husband, writer Richard Michael Levine. Her website is http://lucillelangday.com.

CPSIA information can be obtained
at www.ICGtesting.com
Printed in the USA
FSOW01n1629271215
14798FS